LIVING THINGS

Design	Cooper · West
Editor	Denny Robson
Researcher	Cecilia Weston-Baker
Illustrator	Louise Nevett
Consultant	J. W. Warren Ph.D. Formerly Reader in Physics Education, Department of Physics, Brunel University, London.

© Aladdin Books Ltd

Designed and produced by
Aladdin Books Ltd
70 Old Compton Street
London W1

First published in
Great Britain in 1986 by
Franklin Watts
12a Golden Square
London W1

ISBN 0 86313 437 8

Printed in Belgium

SIMPLY SCIENCE
LIVING THINGS

Kathryn Whyman

FRANKLIN WATTS
London · New York · Toronto · Sydney

INTRODUCTION

Our world is the home of many millions of living things. Living things are found almost everywhere, from the hot, dry deserts to the frozen polar regions, at the bottoms of the oceans, even inside the bodies of other living things! All living things are specially adapted to enable them to survive in their different environments.

Living things, however different they seem to be, share similar needs. In this book you will find out how some of these living things cope with the changes which are constantly taking place around them. You will also discover that all living things depend on each other for their survival.

CONTENTS

What is a living thing?	6
The variety of life	8
Evolution	10
Cells	12
Feeding and breathing	14
Getting from place to place	16
A changing environment	18
Reacting to change	20
Growth and reproduction	22
Communicating	24
Living with each other	26
Make your own "Food Web" game	28
More about reproduction	30
Glossary	31
Index	32

WHAT IS A LIVING THING?

Imagine you were looking at a waxwork model of a child. The model might confuse you at first but you would soon be able to tell that it was not a living thing. A real child can move. A child needs to eat and breathe to survive and get rid of waste materials from its body. A child can see and hear things happening nearby. Eventually the child will grow and may even have children of its own. A model would do none of these things.

The pictures show some living things. They all share some basic characteristics: they need oxygen and "nutrients" for nourishment; they move and grow; they get rid of waste substances and can react to things which happen around them; and they can also reproduce. These are the characteristics of living things.

We can cultivate many forms of plant life in our gardens

Fish are one of the oldest types of living things

THE VARIETY OF LIFE

The world is full of living things. There are about two million different types which exist today! Although they are similar in some ways there are also great differences between them. People have found it useful to sort living things into groups. The two largest groups of living things are the plant and the animal kingdoms. Within these groups there are many different types, or "species", of plants and animals. So scientists divide the plant and animal kingdoms into smaller groups. Animals are divided into those which have backbones, the "vertebrates", and those which do not, the "invertebrates".

Plants have been divided into groups too. The photograph shows just a few of the different types of plant you might find in a woodland.

The animal kingdom
Most animals are invertebrates. For example, earthworms, butterflies, spiders and crabs are just a few invertebrates. Vertebrates can be put into five groups: fish, amphibians (vertebrates which spend part of their lives in water and part on land), birds, reptiles and mammals. Mammals are the only animals which produce milk to feed their young.

Woodland contains many varieties of plant life

EVOLUTION

Where did all the different types of living things come from? Nobody knows for certain but many scientists think that plants and animals have gradually developed, or "evolved", over millions of years. As they have changed they have become better able to survive.

For example, millions of years ago there were many plants but none of them had flowers. Because of small changes in the development of some plants, they began to attract insects which carried pollen to other plants. When pollen is transferred from plant to plant new seeds can develop. Plants which attracted insects were more likely to produce seeds than others which just relied on the wind to carry their pollen. As a result, those plants developed the first simple flowers to attract insects better.

Human beings may have evolved from ape-like animals. They developed the ability to stand upright on just two feet. They could then use their hands for other things. They learnt how to use tools and became successful hunters.

Bees are very efficient flower pollinators

CELLS

All living things are made up of tiny building blocks called "cells". Cells are too small to see without a microscope. The simplest living things have only one cell but the human body consists of about a hundred million million cells!

Almost all cells contain a nucleus. The nucleus is very important as it controls everything that happens inside the cell. Around the nucleus is a jelly-like substance called "cytoplasm". Here lots of chemical reactions take place and some useful chemicals are stored. Around the cytoplasm is a very thin "skin" called the cell membrane. This holds the contents of the cell together and controls what enters and leaves the cell.

Plants and animals have different cells. There are many varieties of plant and animal cells, such as the cells which make up your teeth, skin or hair. They are each designed for a particular job.

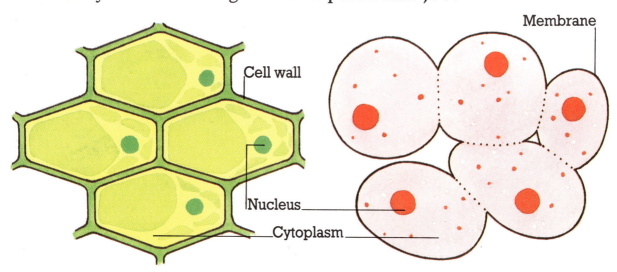

Plant cells
Plant cells are each surrounded by a "cell wall" which gives them support. They each have a nucleus and cytoplasm.

Animal cells
Animals cells have no cell walls as animals use other ways of supporting themselves, such as skeletons.

A leaf under a microscope clearly shows the cell structure

FEEDING AND BREATHING

Living things need certain substances to move, grow and just to keep themselves alive. Animals take in food that is chemically very complicated – plants or animals. This food must be reduced to simpler materials by a process called "digestion". Chemicals inside the body react with the food, breaking it down so that it can be used by the body. Waste materials are excreted.

Plants and animals depend on each other for feeding and breathing. These cabbages take carbon dioxide from the air and water from the soil. In sunlight they convert these simple substances into sugars and starches and produce oxygen. This is "photosynthesis".

Rabbits eat some of the cabbage leaves. They also use the oxygen released by the plants. They produce carbon dioxide which they breathe out. They also get rid of waste water and chemicals from their bodies. All these substances are used by the cabbages.

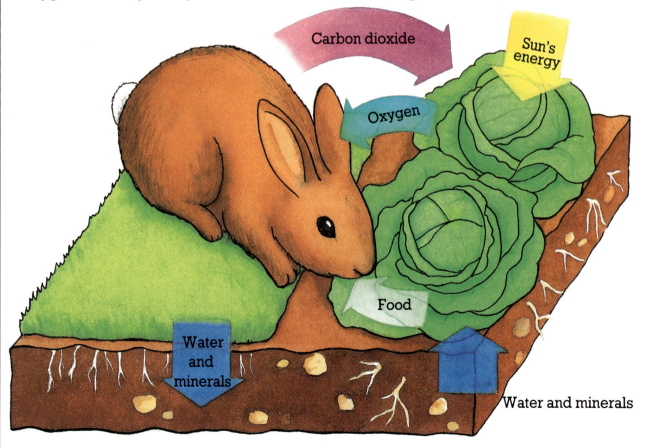

Plants take in simpler substances. The diagram below explains how they manufacture sugars and starches in sunlight. They also need minerals.

Oxygen is necessary to these feeding processes. Animals take in oxygen from the air when they breathe in, and they breathe out carbon dioxide. At night plants also take oxygen from the air. But during the day plants produce their own oxygen – much more than they need. This excess oxygen is released into the air.

Tropical rainforests provide a significant amount of the Earth's oxyen supply

GETTING FROM PLACE TO PLACE

Most animals have to move to find their food. Being able to move also helps them avoid predators and other dangers. Most animals have muscles to help them move. Muscles are parts of the body made up of special cells which can contract (get shorter) and then relax again. Muscles help fish to swim, birds and insects to fly, and many animals to walk and run.

Plants move by growing in different directions. When water is in short supply, plant roots grow deeper into the soil to find it. Shoots grow taller to find more sunlight. Plants also need to move their pollen and seeds. We have seen how pollen is transferred from flower to flower. Seeds must be "dispersed" – spread around – from their parent plant so they have space to grow. They may be carried by animals, water or the wind.

Most snakes get from place to place by throwing their bodies into curves. When a snake moves over land, waves of muscular contraction flow from head to tail. Its sides push against irregularities on the ground (represented by the orange arrows in the diagram).

Creeping plants can spread in many different directions

A CHANGING ENVIRONMENT

Our surroundings are constantly changing. The temperature rises and falls, winds may blow, it may rain, other living things may approach us. Some changes may signal danger to living things. In order to survive, living things must be able to detect changes in their environment and react to them.

It is through our five senses that we can detect changes – sight, smell, hearing, taste and touch. Eyes, ears and noses may detect changes in light, sound or the presence of chemicals for example. Reacting may involve movement. A dog may react to the smell of food by running towards it; an earthworm will react to light by burrowing underground. A chameleon reacts to the threat of danger by using "camouflage" – it changes its skin colour and patterns to match its background.

Plants can react to certain changes in their environment. We have seen how they grow towards light and water. This sunflower gradually turns as it follows the path of the Sun during the day. Some flowers, such as lillies, open during the day and close at night. Plants have no special organs for detecting changes.

This chameleon is well hidden from its predators

REACTING TO CHANGE

When we react to changes, conditions *inside* our bodies change. Sometimes a reaction may be dangerous. For example, if your body temperature increases, as it does during excercise, it must be lowered again quickly. To achieve this, more blood moves to the surface of your skin where it can cool down. Water evaporates from your skin as you sweat – this also cools your body.

It is important to drink after exercise to replace lost fluids

In the winter some animals are no longer able to find food. Changes take place inside their bodies to help them survive this situation, and they "hibernate", like this dormouse. The animal curls up into a ball and "sleeps" for the winter. Its body gradually gets colder and colder. The animal's heartbeat slows down and it breathes less often. In this condition the dormouse uses little energy and so can survive without eating. It lives off stores of fat inside its body.

This dormouse curls up in a hollow log and hibernates during the winter

GROWTH AND REPRODUCTION

As plants and animals develop they get larger and heavier – we say that they grow. How does growth take place? We know that living things take substances into their bodies. Some of these substances are built into the cells. The cells get bigger until they reach a certain size when they cannot grow any more. They then divide into two – from one cell two cells form. As more cells are formed the living thing grows.

When they are fully developed living things can "reproduce". This means they can make new living things similar to themselves. Most living things in the animal world reproduce when special cells called "sex cells" join together, one from the mother and one from the father, forming a "zygote". This zygote grows and divides again and again to form a new living thing.

Simple cell division

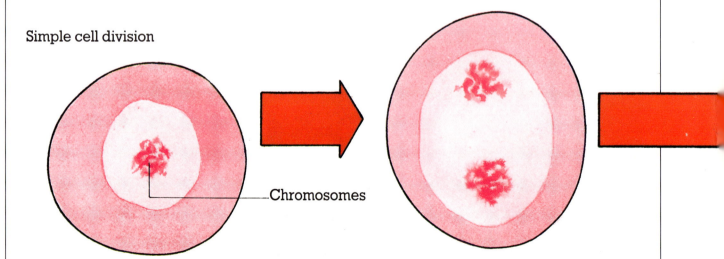

This cell is ready to divide. The threads inside its nucleus, called "chromosomes", have been duplicated. The nucleus now starts to divide. Each new nucleus gets a complete set of chromosomes.

The cell membrane now divides to form two separate cells. These are identical to the original cell with the same number of chromosomes. They will grow and eventually divide into two.

Some mammals, like cats, take only months to become fully developed

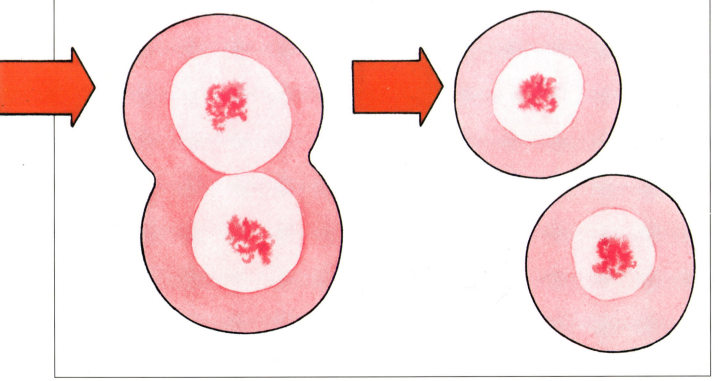

23

COMMUNICATING

Many living things can pass information to each other – they can "communicate". For example they may communicate information about themselves simply by the way they look. The expression on the face of a cat may show that it is angry or frightened.

Some animals communicate by producing chemicals. Cheetahs mark out their territories by spraying urine onto plants. Bees are able to tell each other where to find good sources of food by performing complicated dances. Mammals can show each other affection. Monkeys groom each other and mothers will cuddle their young. Birds and mammals also communicate by making sounds. Humans, as the most intelligent of all animals, have developed the most complicated and successful form of communication – speech.

We usually associate communication with animals, but some plants are also able to communicate. For example, a few trees produce poison in their leaves when they are attacked by insects.

Some of these trees can actually send warning signals to nearby trees. A chemical signal is passed through the air, enabling the trees downwind to prepare for the attack.

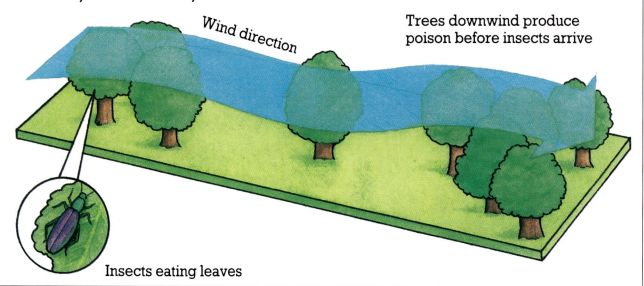

Wind direction

Trees downwind produce poison before insects arrive

Insects eating leaves

Male peacocks, like many birds, display their feathers to attract females and show aggression

LIVING WITH EACH OTHER

A living thing cannot live alone. It depends on other living things to supply it with the materials it needs to survive. We have seen how animals rely on plants for their food. Animals which only eat plants are called "herbivores". Other animals eat herbivores – they are called "carnivores". These carnivores may in turn be eaten by other carnivores. A series of living things which feed on each other make up a "food chain". If one of the members of the chain is removed all the others may be affected.

Often, several food chains interlink as many animals feed on a variety of plants or animals. The chains together make a "food web". Humans eat plants and animals and are usually the last link in a food chain.

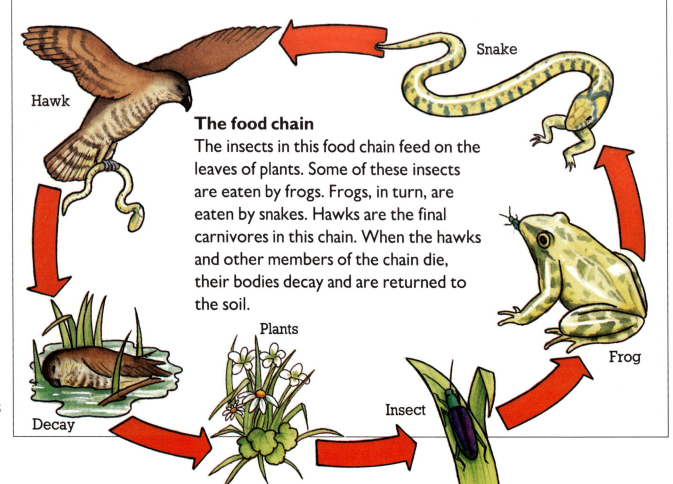

The food chain
The insects in this food chain feed on the leaves of plants. Some of these insects are eaten by frogs. Frogs, in turn, are eaten by snakes. Hawks are the final carnivores in this chain. When the hawks and other members of the chain die, their bodies decay and are returned to the soil.

Coral reefs are part of an elaborate food chain

MAKE YOUR OWN "FOOD WEB" GAME

You can have a lot of fun making and playing this "Food Web" game. You will also learn more about living things and the way they depend on each other for food. All the living things in this game live in Africa. To make the game you will need some card, scissors, tracing paper, pencils, crayons and a ruler. Finally you will need a few friends to play with.

Rules

The game can be played by up to six players. There are 36 cards in the pack. All the players should be dealt an equal number of cards. If there are any cards left over leave them out of the game – but check that MAN is not one of these cards – he MUST be included in the game. The aim of the game is to get rid of your cards as quickly as possible. The winner is the first person to use all his/her cards.

How to play

The person who has MAN starts by placing the card down, face upwards. The players then take their turns in a clockwise direction. Each player must, if possible, put down a card showing a living thing which EITHER eats OR is eaten by the living thing on the previous card. Anyone who cannot go misses their turn. Since in this game MAN eats everything, the second player will always be able to put down a card.

Making the cards

Start by tracing the MAN card. Then look at the diagram below and work out what information to put on the remaining cards. For example, you need to make three WARTHOG cards (shown by the number in brackets). Follow the arrows and you will see that the WARTHOG only eats PLANTS and is eaten by LIONS. Don't forget MAN also eats WARTHOGS!

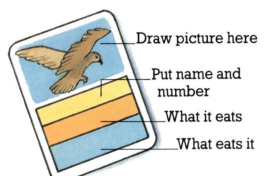

- Draw picture here
- Put name and number
- What it eats
- What eats it

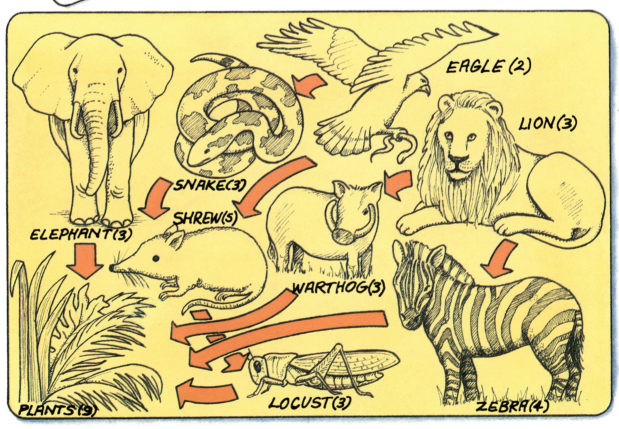

MORE ABOUT REPRODUCTION

Genes and chromosomes
Inside the nucleus of a human cell are 23 pairs of chromosomes. Along these chromosomes are "genes". Genes control everything about you, including the way you look. Each of your cells has the same genes. You got your genes from your parents – half from your mother and half from your father. That is why you look like your parents.

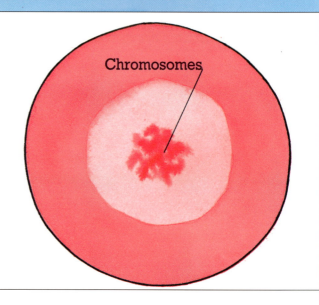

Inheritance
Sex cells have half the usual number of chromosomes. This father's sex cells carry a gene for brown eyes and the mother's a gene for blue. Their children receive both sets of information, but they all have brown eyes – the brown gene is "dominant". The cells of these brown-eyed parents each have genes for brown and blue eyes. Half their sex cells get genes for brown eyes and half get genes for blue. Their children will have brown eyes *unless* two sex cells carrying genes for blue eyes join together.

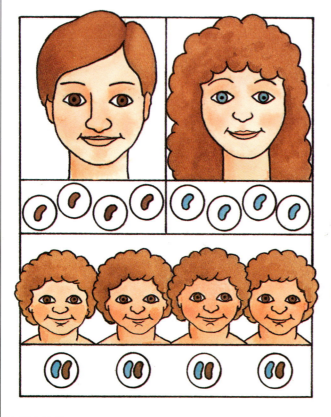
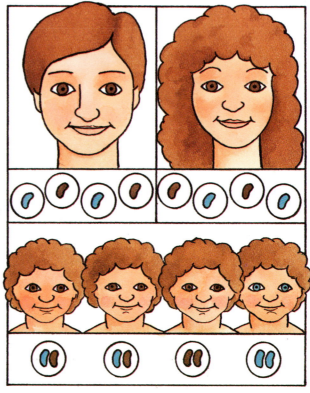

GLOSSARY

Camouflage
Disguise of colour or patterns that hides an animal.

Carbon dioxide
A colourless gas found in the air. It is essential for plants to make sugars and starches.

Disperse
To scatter or spread around. Seeds are dispersed to give them a better chance of survival.

Dominant
Used to describe a gene if the information it carries is always expressed in a living thing, even if only one of its type is present in a cell.

Evaporate
To change a liquid into a gas. A liquid needs energy to evaporate and so absorbs heat from its surroundings.

Hibernation
Winter sleep when an animal's temperature lowers and heartbeat slows.

Minerals
Substances in soil water (for plants) or in food (for animals) which are needed for growth.

Nutrient
A substance which provides nourishment, such as minerals.

Oxygen
A colourless gas which makes up about a fifth of the air. It is essential to the lives of plants and animals.

Pollen
Fine dust produced by the male part of a plant, usually in the flower. It contains the male sex cells of the plant.

Sex cell
A cell which has to join with another cell before it will develop into a new plant or animal. It is also called a "gamete".

Skeleton
The hard parts of an animal which support its body. They may be on the outside of the body (such as the shell of a crab) or on the inside (such as the bones of a cat).

Species
A group of plants or animals which are like each other and which can reproduce together. For example all dogs belong to the same species.

Urine
The watery liquid which carries waste substances out of the bodies of some animals.

Zygote
A cell formed by the joining together of a male and female sex cell. In the right conditions a zygote will develop and grow into a new living thing.

INDEX

A
air 14, 15, 31
amphibian 8
animals 8, 10, 12, 14, 15, 16, 21, 22, 24, 26, 31

B
birds 8, 16, 24, 25
bodies 6, 12, 14, 16, 20, 21, 22, 26, 31
breathing 6, 14, 15, 21

C
camouflage 18, 19, 31
carbon dioxide 14, 15, 31
carnivores 26
cells 12-13, 16, 22, 30, 31
chromosomes 22, 30
communications 24

D
digestion 14

E
eating 6, 14, 21, 26
evolution 6, 14
excretion 6, 14, 31

F
fish 7, 8, 16
flowers 10, 11, 16, 18
food 14, 21, 24, 26, 27, 28, 31

G
genes 30, 31
growth 6, 14, 22, 31

H
herbivores 26
hibernation 21, 31
human beings 10, 12, 24, 26, 30

I
insects 8, 10, 16, 24, 26
invertebrates 8

M
mammals 8, 23, 24
minerals 14, 15, 31
movement 6, 14, 16

N
nutrients 6, 31

O
oxygen 6, 14, 15, 31

P
photosynthesis 14
plants 6, 8, 9, 10, 12, 14, 15, 16, 18, 22, 24, 26, 31
pollination 10, 11

R
reproduction 6, 22, 30, 31
reptiles 8

S
seeds 10, 16, 31
senses 6, 18
skeleton 12, 31
soil 14, 16, 26, 31
sunlight 14, 15, 16, 18
survival 6, 10, 18, 21, 23, 26, 31

V
vertebrates 8

W
water 14, 16, 18, 20, 31

Photographic Credits:
Cover: Bruce Colman; title page, contents page and pages 9, 11, 15 and 25: Zefa; pages 6, 13 and 20: Picturepoint; page 7: Spectrum; page 17: Susan Griggs; page 19: Ardea; page 21: Planet Earth; page 23: Art Directors; page 27: Tony Stone.